MINERALS AND GEMS

FROM THE AMERICAN MUSEUM OF NATURAL HISTORY

MINERALS
AND GEMS

FROM THE AMERICAN MUSEUM
OF NATURAL HISTORY

George E. Harlow
Joseph J. Peters

A TINY FOLIO™
ABBEVILLE PRESS PUBLISHERS
New York • London • Paris

Front cover: Elbaites in different colors, including a superb bicolored crystal 10.5 cm (4½ in.) high from Tourmaline Queen Mine, San Diego County, Pala, California.
Back Cover: Azurite and Malachite (Polished Slice). See page 104.
Spine: Rock Crystal Carving of a Horse Head. See page 280.
Page 1: Left: The "Patricia Emerald," Colombia, 629 carats, 6.6 cm (1½ in.) high.
Right: The "Schettler Emerald." See page 233.
Page 2: Gemstone crystals including tourmaline, aquamarine, emerald, morganite, heliodor, topaz, kunzite, spodumene and citrine.
Page 5: Left: Quartz (Variety Amethyst); Hopkinton, Rhode Island; Scepter crystal 4 cm (1⅜ in.) across. Right: Faceted gems, including topaz, amethyst, aquamarine, morganite, chrysoberyl, peridot, smoky quartz, citrine, calcite, rhodochrosite, and fluorite. Sizes range from 14.91 to 454 carats.

Editor: Susan Costello
Designer: Sandy Burne
Production Editor: Abigail Asher
Production Supervisor: Simone René

Library of Congress Cataloging-in-Publication Data
American Museum of Natural History.
    Minerals and gems : from the American Museum of Natural History /
George E. Harlow, Joseph J. Peters.
    p.   cm.
    Includes index.
    ISBN 1-55859-273-3 (pbk.)
    1. Minerals—Catalogs and collections—New York (N.Y.) 2. Precious stones—Catalogs
and collections—New York (N.Y.) 3. American Museum of Natural History—Catalogs.
I. Harlow, George E. II. Peters, Joseph J. III. Title
    QE386.U62N493 1994
    549'.074'7471—dc20
                                     94-10365

CONTENTS

INTRODUCTION

Minerals are the foundation of the earth, the very stuff upon
which we walk. We mine, cut, crush, roast, smelt, and refine them.
When transformed they become roads, bridges, cars, buildings,
computers, statues, ceramics, medicines, gems, and much more.

Minerals can be exceedingly beautiful and exquisite in their geometric perfection as crystals. Those who are unaware of nature's
order might easily mistake a crystal for an object crafted by hand.
Since many cultures believe only gods could create such perfection,
it is not surprising that many attribute transcendental powers to
crystals. Minerals have been collected as objects of curiosity, beauty,
and ornamentation; for their talismanic or curative powers; and as
scientific specimens that document the diversity of nature and the
organization of matter.

Natural history museums are the major repositories and
archives for minerals and related natural resources. These museums
display them and explain the science and importance of minerals.
This book illustrates a small fraction of the specimens in the collections of the American Museum of Natural History in New York City,
focusing on their beauty, the perfection of their crystals, and the

qualities that make each outstanding or unique. In these pictures you will find an enticing introduction to mineralogy and gemology and a window into some of the museum's many treasures.

WHAT ARE MINERALS?

It's easy to appreciate the beauty of minerals and gems, but understanding what they are requires some background. A mineral is usually defined as a naturally occurring, inorganic crystalline solid with a chemical composition that can be defined by a chemical formula (for example, SiO_2—one silicon atom per two oxygens). The criterion "naturally occurring" eliminates artificial fabrications such as the synthetic diamond simulant cubic zirconia. Precipitation from water is an example of an inorganic process that produces minerals. Rocks, sand, soil, and sediments are composed of minerals. Although formed biologically, plants and animals utilize minerals in their bodies: tooth enamel contains apatite, clam shells aragonite, and the serrations in grass blades even contain quartz phytoliths.

In a crystalline solid, the constituent atoms are organized into a regularly repeating solid network that could be compared to a three-dimensional version of a geometric wallpaper pattern. In each portion of a crystal, the atoms are identically arranged. This regularity leads to the formation of bodies defined by natural flat faces, which is the hallmark of a crystal. Since crystal growth is usually confined by neighboring formations, well-formed specimens are relatively uncommon. Nonetheless, these irregular bodies are still crystals. In rocks and soils, minerals can be too small to see with an unaided eye, hiding both the well-formed crystal and the irregular grain.

A crystal is held together by bonds—attractive forces between adjacent atoms. The combination of bonds and the chemical identity of the atoms give a crystal all of its properties, including hardness, durability, cleavage, density, refractive index, magnetism, melting point, and thermal and electrical conductivity. Minerals are the natural analogues of all crystalline solids, so mineralogists (those who study minerals) share interests with ceramists, metallurgists, physicists, and others interested in solid matter. Minerals are often the basis for creation of synthetic materials that are essential to our technologically advanced society. For example, zeolites (aluminosilicates with large ion exchange cavities) are used as catalysts for "cracking" thick crude oil into gasoline. Moreover, an understanding of minerals makes it easier to understand the greater physical world.

For centuries, people have appreciated one fundamental aspect of crystals and minerals, namely the symmetry possessed by the crystals and their atomic arrangement. There are three basic forms of symmetry: mirror, rotation, and inversion. Our hands are an example of mirror symmetry. Objects in rotational symmetry can be rotated a discrete angle yet appear unchanged; in crystals this is restricted to one-half, one-third, one-fourth, and one-sixth of a full rotation. Finally, in inversion symmetry every part of an object is related to the opposite side as if connected by a line through a central point. For example, a cube has a center of symmetry but a pyramid does not. For crystals, there are thirty-two possible combinations of mirror, rotation, and inversion symmetry.

A crystal expresses the symmetry and the basic dimensional relationships of the atoms from which it is constructed. It can be likened to a stack of minute bricks, each brick with an identical shape and set of dimensions. While crystals can have great individuality of shape, the range of symmetry is greatly constrained: there are only seven basic systems of symmetry (see the diagrams on the following pages). Determining the symmetry of a crystal, usually by inspection, is a powerful tool in identification.

In this book and in a large section of the Mineral Hall at the Museum of Natural History, minerals are organized according to the Dana system, named after its nineteenth-century originators James B. Dana and Edward S. Dana. The Dana system organizes mineral species based on the chemical composition and atomic arrangement of their crystals—their crystal structures. An organizational method is necessary both to categorize mineral diversity and to understand the underlying principles of nature's organization. The Dana system begins with the compositionally simplest substances, the native

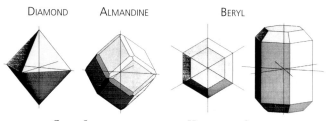

DIAMOND   ALMANDINE   BERYL

CUBIC SYSTEM:
3 equal perpendicular axes

HEXAGONAL SYSTEM:
One 6-fold axis

BENITOITE   ZIRCON

TRIGONAL SYSTEM:
One 3-fold axis

TETRAGONAL SYSTEM:
2 equal axes, all perpendicular

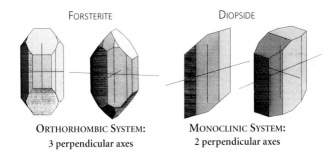

FORSTERITE

DIOPSIDE

ORTHORHOMBIC SYSTEM:
3 perpendicular axes

MONOCLINIC SYSTEM:
2 perpendicular axes

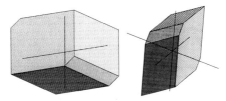

MANGANAXINITE

TRICLINIC SYSTEM:
No restrictions on axes

elements, which have a single chemical constituent such as carbon in diamond, and progresses to complex compounds containing a metal and an oxygen-bearing anionic group. For example, calcite is a form of calcium carbonate, where calcium is the metal and carbonate is a carbon-oxygen anion.

Crystal structure permits another level of distinction that is especially necessary for distinguishing different minerals that have the same chemical composition. For example, diamond and graphite are both composed of carbon; calcite and aragonite are both calcium carbonate. Mineral groups are made up of different minerals that share the same fundamental structure.

What Are Gems?

Gems are minerals with natural beauty—color, transparency, brilliance, or iridescence—that have been cut, ground, and polished to enhance their beauty so that they can be used in objects of adornment. Rubies, sapphires, and emeralds are the colorful cousins of the minerals found in ordinary rocks. Some materials that are considered to be gems, like pearls and amber, are natural but they are not minerals.

Gems used for jewelry, especially those used in rings, must endure wear. To resist being scratched, the ideal gem must be hard; to resist being broken, it must be durable. Many beautiful minerals cannot be used as gems because they could not survive in a piece of jewelry. Other criteria that help determine the quality or suitability of a gem are transparency, clarity, and the evenness and depth of color. The raw gemstone must also be large enough to fashion, rare enough to distinguish it from the ordinary, yet not so rare as to be unavailable and unmarketable.

Just as gems fascinate the public, so do they fascinate mineralogists and geoscientists because of their unusual or superlative nature. We ask how, why, where, and when did they form so large and perfectly, or what is the source of their color and sparkle. Gems are also a wonderful introduction to the optical and physical properties they manifest and the way our human perception figures into their appearance and appeal.

Gems present a problem for classification because beyond the system for minerals there is no objective criterion for organizing gems. Personal taste and commercial value are appropriate criteria, but they are not objective and they vary with time and fashion. Traditionally, the terms "precious" and "semiprecious" have been used to separate diamonds, emeralds, rubies, and sapphires from all other gems, but the distinction is not particularly valid in terms of monetary value. The "big four" are nonetheless the most popular and dominant stones, and they retain their hierarchical position by beginning the gem section in this book. However, we have grouped the other beryl gems—aquamarine, heliodor, and morganite—with emerald in order to keep all the gems of the same mineral species together. The other gems and ornamental materials are presented by mineral species or mineral group in an order clustering similar gems together. Otherwise they present the tastes of the authors. To each his own!

TERMINOLOGY

The terms used in the captions require some explanation. Minerals grow naturally in association and contact with one another. If one crystal grows "on" another, the former is perched on the surface of the latter; an example is hematite on quartz. Hematite "with" quartz indicates adjacent crystals of the two species. Hematite "in" quartz signifies that the quartz encapsulates the hematite crystal or crystals. A "twinned crystal" indicates that two or more crystals of the same mineral are intergrown in a precise geometric relationship that would not be permitted by the mineral's actual symmetry. Twins can create fascinating forms. Finally, "variety" names are sometimes given to minor variations in a mineral's composition, color, or crystal shape. For example, ruby is the blood-red variety of corundum as well as the name of the gem. The captions give sizes in both centimeters and inches. Gem weights are given in carats; one gram equals five carats.

THE AMERICAN MUSEUM OF NATURAL HISTORY

The American Museum of Natural History was founded in 1869, when New York City was forging its position as financial and mercantile capital of the United States and establishing its cultural and educational leadership. The museum's founder, Albert S. Bickmore, reasoned that a great museum of natural history belonged in the country's greatest city. Engaging the support of prominent New Yorkers like T. R. Roosevelt (the future president's father), J. Pierpont

Morgan, Morris K. Jessup, and A. G. Phelps and William Dodge (of the Phelps-Dodge Copper Corporation), Bickmore was given the second floor of Central Park's Arsenal Building to create his museum. Within two years, the construction of the museum's permanent home was underway, and it eventually grew to the present enclave of twenty-three buildings, forming the largest natural history museum complex in the world.

At first the mineral and gem collection was small, but it has grown continuously over its 125-year history. Some major additions deserve mention. George F. Kunz, from 1879 to 1930 the legendary gemologist of Tiffany & Co., always favored the American Museum of Natural History. He assembled two prize-winning collections of minerals and precious stones that came to the museum. Kunz created a magnificent collection of North American gems and precious stones as one of Tiffany's entries into the Paris Exposition Universelle of 1889. It was ultimately purchased for the museum by trustee J. Pierpont Morgan. For the Paris Exposition Universelle of 1900, Morgan gave Kunz carte blanche to create a similar collection of specimens, this time specimens not of American origin. The collection, which received a grand prize at the Exposition, came to the museum in 1901 to form the combined Morgan-Tiffany collection of, in Kunz's words, "2,176 specimens of gemstones, objects of precious stone, and 2,442 pearls."

Also in 1901, Morgan purchased and donated the superb mineral collection of Clarence S. Bement, a Philadelphia industrialist. Bement had acquired among the finest specimens of every mineral species, amassing about 12,000 minerals and 580 meteorites. This 100,000-dollar purchase required several boxcars to transport it to New York. In an instant, it created the finest museum mineral collection in the Americas. More minerals and gems came from Morgan, including the 563-carat Star of India, the world's largest fine star sapphire. Later Pierpont's son, Jack Morgan, continued the tradition, in particular with his donation of a phenomenal suite of large sapphires. A major bequest of minerals and carvings came to the museum in 1952 from the estate of William Boyce Thompson, founder of the Newmont Mining Corporation, along with an endowment that enables the museum to acquire new specimens. The last, but largest, addition to the mineral collection was the acquisition of the Columbia University Systematic Mineral Collection in 1980. This diverse assemblage of some 40,000 specimens nearly doubled the size of the extant collections. The present collections include about 98,000 minerals and 2,800 gems, carvings, and pieces of gem-bearing jewelry.

The minerals and gems have been displayed in several different exhibition spaces in the museum. Prior to 1974, the cavernous J. Pierpont Morgan Memorial Hall of Minerals and Gems on the fourth floor was the display and storage area. It was in this hall that the infamous gem heist by Jack "Murph-the-Surf" Murphy and two co-conspirators occurred in 1964. Allegedly inspired by the film *Topkapi* about a fictitious robbery from that Istanbul museum, the perpetrators made a daring window entry from the floor above and made off with most of the diamonds and large gems. All of the large stones were eventually recovered, but a number of emeralds and all of the diamonds were never returned—a real tragedy, especially considering the irreplaceable American origin of many of the diamonds. Needless to say, security was improved thereafter, particularly in the design of the collections' next home.

In 1976, the present Harry F. Guggenheim Hall of Minerals and the J. P. Morgan Memorial Hall of Gems on the museum's first floor was opened. A daring departure from traditional museum design, the earthy-brown multi-leveled interior, the brightly illuminated exhibit cases, and the free-standing specimens evoke a subterranean cache of mineral wealth. The halls include areas on systematics and properties, mineral forming environments, and a video theater that combines education with the presentation of the museum's world-class collections. More than 300 photographs here provide an exciting introduction to the 2,500 mineral specimens and the 1,000 gems and objets d'art on exhibit.

MINERAL AND GEM PHOTOGRAPHS

Photographing mineral and gem specimens requires special talents. The exciting qualities that people observe in crystals and gems—combinations of color, luster, reflection, transparency, form, texture, and contrast—are exceedingly difficult to record on film. Unlike photos of paintings, where the painting is the work of art, here both the specimens and the photographs are art, one created by nature, the other by the photographer.

Over the years we have been fortunate to work with photographers who are very accomplished in the portraiture of minerals and gems. Thus, this guide to mineral and gem treasures at the American Museum of Natural History is also a tribute to their photography. The principal photography was done by Harold and Erica Van Pelt and Jackie Beckett. Additional photographs were taken by Arthur Singer, Jim Coxe, Olivia Bauer, Kerry Perkins, Emil Javorsky, Herb Speiselman, and others. Individual credits are given at the end of the book.

MINERALS

The minerals are presented essentially according to the Dana system, which classifies them by their chemical composition and crystal structure. In simple terms, this places the metals and metallic minerals (elements, sulfides, tellurides, and the like) at the beginning, and most of the rock-forming minerals (quartz, feldspars, pyroxenes) at the end, but ultimately chemistry reigns. Except for minerals described in the early days of mineralogy, when morphological names were used in the taxonomic style of Linnaeus and modern biologists, minerals are basically named after people (usually scientists) and places. Although there are a few chemical prefixes, suffixes, and compositional acronyms, names are not helpful to understanding or remembering what minerals are. Thus, for example, franklinite, a zinc iron oxide, is named for its source at Franklin, New Jersey, and willemite, a zinc silicate, is named after King Willem Frederik of the Netherlands. The chart below gives the minerals in order of their presentation. The numbers following each mineral refer to pages.

25-Carat Octahedral Diamond Crystal in Kimberlite
Premier Mine, Kimberley, South Africa
On loan from Mrs. Charles W. Engelhard

Single and Twinned Diamond Crystals
Arkansas, Zaire, South Africa, and Unknown Localities
Largest crystal 1 cm (⅜ in.)

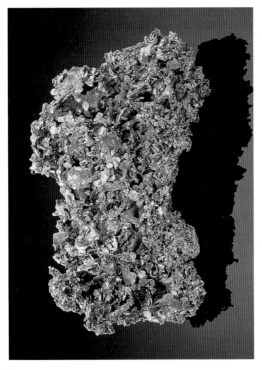

"Newmont" Native Gold
Empire-Star Mines, Grass Valley, California
18.8 cm (7½ in.) across

Native Gold
Byrd's Valley, Placer County, California
12 cm (4 ¾ in.) across

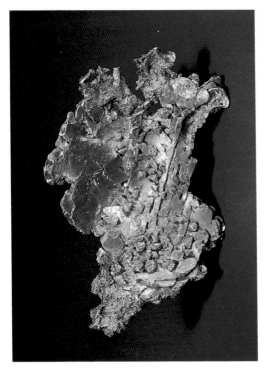

Native Gold on Quartz
Placerville, California
9.5 cm (3¾ in.) across

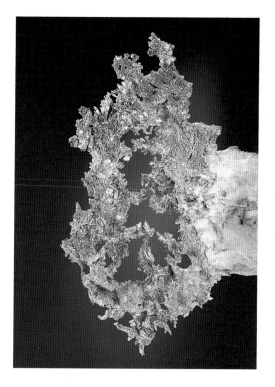

Native Gold in Quartz
Eagle's Nest Mine, Placer County, California
14.5 cm (5¾ in.) across

Native Gold Sheet on Quartz
El Dorado County, California
5 cm (2 in.) high

Native Gold "Latticework" Crystal
California
5.7 cm (2¼ in.) across

Native Gold on Matrix
Santiam Mine, Oregon
3 cm (1⅛ in.) across

Native Gold
Colorado
7.5 cm (3 in.) across

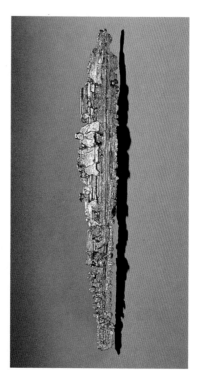

Native Gold
Colorado
3 cm (1⅛ in.) long

Native Gold (Variety Electrum)
Rosia-Montana, Romania
Central crystal 1 cm (⅜ in.) across

Native Copper
Lake Superior, Michigan
30.4 cm (12 in.) across

Native Copper in Calcite
Hancock, Houghton County, Michigan
12 cm (4¾ in.) across

Native Copper
Cornwall, England
12 cm (4¾ in.) across

Native Copper
Cornwall, England
2.5 cm (1 in.) high

Native Silver and Copper (Half-breed)
Lake Superior, Michigan
25.5 cm (10 in.) high

Native Silver with Calcite
Kongsberg, Norway
10 cm (4 in.) across

Sulfur on Aragonite
Agrigento, Sicily
Largest crystal 3 cm (1⅛ in.) across

Chalcocite on Rock Matrix
Bristol, Connecticut
Largest crystals 2 cm (¾ in.) long

Chalcocite
Cornwall, England
7 cm (2 ¾ in.) across

Pyrite in Shale
Springfield, Illinois
7 cm (2 ¾ in.) diameter

Pyrite
Huanzala, Peru
12.8 cm (5 in.) across

Marcasite
Galena, Illinois
11.5 cm (4½ in.) across

Marcasite
Pitcher, Oklahoma
Crystals 17.5 cm (6 ⅞ in.) across

Chalcopyrite on Quartz
Cambourne, Cornwall, England
Largest crystals 3 cm (1⅛ in.) long

Chalcopyrite on Quartz
Callington, England
12.5 cm (5 in.) across

Twinned Cubanite Crystal on Limestone
Chibougamau, Quebec, Canada
Crystal 2 cm (¾ in.) across

Carrollite on Calcite
Kambove Mine, Shaba Province, Zaire
9.2 cm (3⅝ in.) across

Millerite with Hematite and Quartz
Antwerp, New York
9.5 cm (3¾ in.) across

Galena on Quartz with Siderite
Neudorf, Harz, Germany
Galena 6.3 cm (2½ in.) across

Galena with Calcite
Marsden's Diggings, Galena, Illinois
7.5 cm (3 in.) across

Galena with Calcite
Rossie, New York
12 cm (4 ¾ in.) across

Cinnabar on Quartz
Hunan Province, China
Crystal 2.5 cm (1 in.) across

Stibnite
Ichinokawa, Iyo, Japan
Crystals 26 cm (10 in.) high

Stibnite
Baia Sprie, Romania
23 cm (9 in.) across

Calaverite on Quartz
Cripple Creek, Colorado
Crystal 1.3 cm (½ in.) high

Hessite
Botes, Romania
2.6 cm (1 in.) high

Halite on Rock Matrix
Krakow Salt Works, Wieliczka, Poland
18 cm (7 in.) across

Boleite on Rock Matrix
Boleo, Baja California, Mexico
11.5 cm (4½ in.) across

Matlockite
Matlock, Derbyshire, England
9.5 cm (3¾ in.) across

Fluorite
Westmoreland, New Hampshire
Crystal 25 cm (10 in.) along an edge

Fluorite on Sphalerite
Elmwood Mine, Carthage, Tennessee
Crystals 2.5 cm (1 in.) across

Fluorite
Denton Mine, Hardin County, Illinois
8.3 cm (3 ¼ in.) high

Fluorite
Muquiz, Coahuila, Mexico
Matrix 15 cm (6 in.) across

Fluorite
Stak Nala, Gilgit, Pakistan
Crystal 6 cm (2 ⅜ in.) across

Fluorite on Rock Matrix
Göschenen, Switzerland
Crystals 1.5 cm (⅝ in.) across

Cuprite with Green Malachite Coating
Onganja, Namibia
10 cm (4 in.) across

Zincite in Calcite
Franklin, New Jersey
15 cm (6 in.) across

Zincite in Marble
Franklin, New Jersey
Crystal 1.2 cm (½ in.) across

Corundum (Variety Ruby) in White Marble
Jagdalak, Afghanistan
Crystal 4 cm (1½ in.) long

Intergrown Water-worn Corundum (Variety Sapphire) Crystals
Sri Lanka
5 cm (2 in.) long

Hematite on Quartz
St. Gothard, Switzerland
10.5 cm (4 ⅛ in.) across

Hematite
Cleator Moor, Cumberland, England
1 m (3 ft.) across

Bixbyite on Rhyolite
Thomas Range, Utah
Largest crystal 1 cm (⅜ in.) across

Paramelaconite with Footeite and Cuprite
Copper Queen Mine, Bisbee, Arizona
Largest crystal 7.5 cm (3 in.)

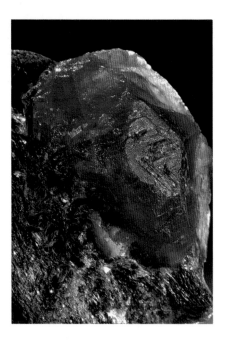

Twinned Chrysoberyl (Variety Alexandrite)
Illuminated with incandescent light
Malysheva Mine, Takovaya, Urals, Russia
Crystal 3.7 cm (1½ in.)

Twinned Chrysoberyl (Variety Alexandrite)
Same specimen illuminated with sunlight
Malysheva Mine, Takovaya, Urals, Russia
Crystal 3.7 cm (1½ in.) across

Twinned Chrysoberyl
Espirito Santo, Brazil
8 cm (3⅛ in.) across

Spinel on Rock Matrix
Amity, New York
12.5 cm (5 in.) across

Gahnite in Calcite
Franklin, New Jersey
Crystal 2.5 cm (1 in.) on an edge

Magnetite with Chondrodite and Calcite
Tilly Foster Mine, Brewster, New York
12 cm (4¾ in.) across

Magnetite on Rock Matrix
Binnenthal, Switzerland
Crystal 1.7 cm (⅔ in.) on an edge

Franklinite
Franklin, New Jersey
Largest crystal 3.2 cm (1¼ in.) across

Manganite
Ilfeld, Harz, Germany
15 cm (6 in.) across

Columbite with Feldspar and Mica
Rincon district, San Diego County, California
Black crystal 3.5 cm (1⅜ in.) long

Stibiotantalite with Elbaite, Lepidolite, and Feldspar
Stewart Mine, Pala, San Diego County, California
5 cm (2 in.) across

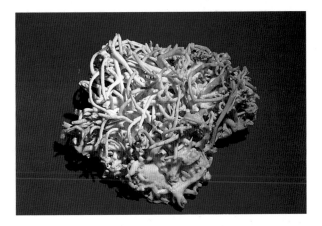

Aragonite (Variety Flos Feri)
Eisenerz, Styria, Austria
12 cm (4¾ in.) across

Calcite on Sphalerite
Elmwood Mine, Carthage, Tennessee
11.5 cm (4½ in.) across

Calcite
Elmwood Mine, Carthage, Tennessee
21 cm (8 ¼ in.) across

Calcite on Rock Matrix
Sweetwater Mine, Reynolds County, Missouri
Crystal 10 cm (4 in.) long

Calcite on Rock Matrix
Sweetwater Mine, Reynolds County, Missouri
Crystal 17.5 cm (6 ⅞ in.) long

Calcite on Amethyst
Guanajuato, Mexico
12.5 cm (5 in.) across

Rhodochrosite
Home Sweet Home Mine, Alma, Colorado
12.3 cm (4 ⅞ in.) across

Siderite on Quartz
Tincroft Mine, Redruth, Cornwall, England
Crystals average 0.5 cm (¼ in.)

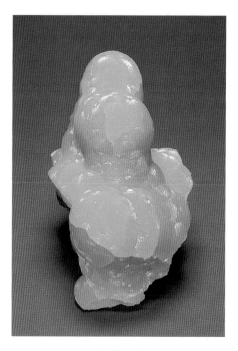

Smithsonite
Kelly Mine, Magdalena, New Mexico
10.5 cm (4 in.) across

Cerussite on Rock Matrix
Tsumeb, Namibia
14.5 cm (5 ¾ in.) across

"Newmont" Azurite on Rock Matrix
Tsumeb Mine, Tsumeb, Namibia
Largest crystal 20 cm. (8 in.) long

Azurite
Copper Queen Mine, Bisbee, Arizona
20 cm (8 in.) across

Azurite and Malachite Block
Copper Queen Mine, Bisbee, Arizona
2.6 m (5 ft.) high, 4½ tons

Azurite and Malachite (Polished Slice)
Clifton, Arizona
7.5 cm (3 in.) in diameter

Azurite and Malachite
Bisbee, Arizona
16.5 cm (6½ in.) high

Azurite and Malachite
Bisbee, Arizona
16.5 cm (6½ in.) high

Malachite
Copper Queen Mine, Bisbee, Arizona
20 cm (8 in.) across

Parisite in Calcite
Muzo, Colombia
Crystal 2 cm (¾ in.) long

Anhydrite
Simplon Tunnel, St. Gothard, Switzerland
5.7 cm (2¼ in.) across

Gypsum (Variety Selenite)
Santa Eulalia, Chihuahua, Mexico
18 cm (7 in.) across

Anglesite in Galena
Wheatley Mine, Phoenixville, Pennsylvania
7.5 cm (3 in.) across

Barite on Calcite
Near Meade, South Dakota
15.7 cm (6 ⅛ in.) across

Barite
Frizington, Cumberland, England
Crystal 10 cm (4 in.) across

Barite
Santa Lucia, Sardinia
7.5 cm (3 in.) across

Barite (Stained by Realgàr)
Baia Sprie, Romania
6.3 cm (2½ in.) across

Celestine
Lime City, Ohio
29 cm (11⅜ in.) across

Brazilianite
Conselheira Pena, Minas Gerais, Brazil
10 cm (4 in.) across

Fluorapatite with Cookeite
Pulsifer Quarry, Auburn, Maine
Purple crystal 2.5 cm (1 in.) high

Fluorapatite with Muscovite and Albite
Dusso, Gilgit, Pakistan
Pink crystal 3 cm (1⅛ in.) across

Fluorapatite
Lavra da Ilha, Minas Gerais, Brazil
4 cm (1½ in.) across

Pyromorphite
Bunker Hill Mine, Kellogg, Idaho
7.7 cm (3 in.) across

Pyromorphite
Bunker Hill Mine, Kellogg, Idaho
5 cm (2 in.) across

Vanadinite on Rock Matrix
Mibladen, Morocco
36 cm (14 in.) across

Hydroxylherderite
Blue Chihuahua Mine, San Diego County, California
Crystal 3.5 cm (1⅜ in.) long

Hydroxylherderite
Virgem da Lapa, Minas Gerais, Brazil
10 cm (4 in.) across

Hydroxylherderite with Fluorapatite and Albite
Dusso, Gilgit, Pakistan
Green crystal 2 cm (¾ in.) across

Lazulite in Sandstone
Graves Mountain, Lincoln County, Georgia
7 cm (2 ¾ in.) across

Chalcosiderite on Limonite
Wheal Phoenix, Cornwall, England
8 cm (3¼ in.) across

Roselite (Pink Crystals) on Calcite
Bou Azzer, Morocco
Average crystal .5 cm (³⁄₁₆ in.) long

Adamite on Limonite
Mapimi, Durango, Mexico
7.5 cm (3 in.) across

Legrandite
Mapimi, Durango, Mexico
Crystal spray 23 cm (9 in.) long

Vivianite with Marcasite
Morococala, Oruro, Bolivia
11.5 cm (4½ in.) across

Erythrite on Rock Matrix
Schneeburg, Saxony, Germany
10 cm (4 in.) across

Liroconite with Quartz and Limonite
Wheal Unity Mine, Cornwall, England
Largest crystal 1.3 cm (½ in.) long

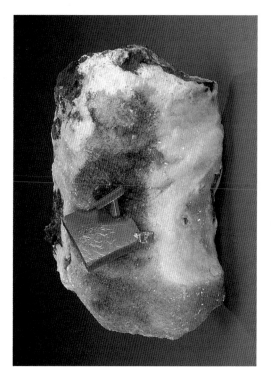

Wulfenite on Chalcedony
Los Lamentos, Chihuahua, Mexico
10 cm (4 in.) across

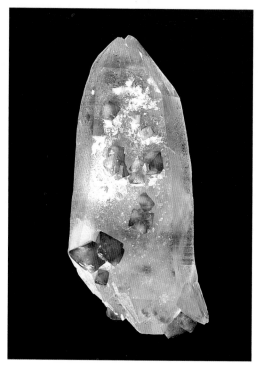

Scheelite on Quartz
Tae Wha Mine, Neungam-Ri, Korea
10 cm (4 in.) across

Scheelite with Quartz
Tae Wha Mine, Neungam-Ri, Korea
10 cm (4 in.) across

Willemite (White "Balls") in Massive Willemite (Brown)
Franklin, New Jersey
12.5 cm (5 in.) across

Willemite
Same specimen illuminated with shortwave ultra-violet light
Franklin, New Jersey
12.5 cm (5 in.) across

Willemite (Brown) in Calcite (White)
Sterling Hill Mine, Ogdensburg, New Jersey
11 cm (4⅜ in.) across

Same specimen illuminated with shortwave ultra-violet light:
Willemite (Green) in Calcite (Pink)
Sterling Hill Mine, Ogdensburg, New Jersey
11 cm (4⅜ in.) across

Almandine Garnet
Russell, Massachusetts
6 cm (2 ⅜ in.) across

Spessartine Garnet with Muscovite and Quartz
Leiper's Quarry, Springfield Township, Pennsylvania
Two intergrown crystals 5 cm (2 in.) across

Spessartine Garnet on Smoky Quartz
Ramona, California
Crystal 1.5 cm (⅝ in.) across

Spessartine Garnet with Albite
Gilgit, Pakistan
7.5 cm (3 in.) across

Titanite with Chlorite
Tilly Foster Mine, Brewster, New York
Crystals 1.5 cm (⅝ in.) across

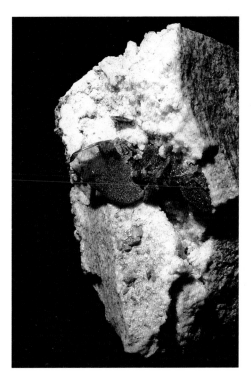

Titanite with Chlorite
Velver-Tauern, Austria
10 cm (4 in.) across

Hodgkinsonite with Franklinite, Calcite, and Willemite
Franklin, New Jersey
5.5 cm (2¼ in.) across

Chondrodite in Marble
Tilly Foster Mine, Brewster, New York
Large crystal 3 cm (1¼ in.) across

Norbergite in Calcite
Franklin, New Jersey
11 cm (4⅜ in.) across

Topaz with Microcline
Little Three Mine, Ramona, San Diego County, California
5 cm (2 in.) across

Topaz
Little Three Mine, Ramona, San Diego County, California
5 cm (2 in.) across

Topaz in Rhyolite
Thomas Range, Utah
Crystal 2.2 cm (⅞ in.) high

The World's Largest Topaz Crystal
Fazenda do Funil, Minas Gerais, Brazil
271 kg (596 lb.)

Topaz with Quartz
Dusso, Gilgit, Pakistan
Crystal 2.5 cm (1 in.) high

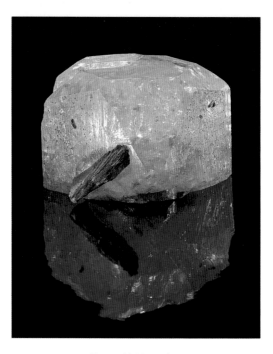

Topaz with Muscovite
Mursinka, Urals, Russia
Crystal 10.5 cm (4¼ in.) high

Topaz
Wolinskii Wolin, Ukraine
Crystal 19.5 cm (7 ⅝ in.) high

Zoisite (Variety Tanzanite)
Merelani Mine, Arusha, Tanzania
4.2 cm (1⅝ in.) high

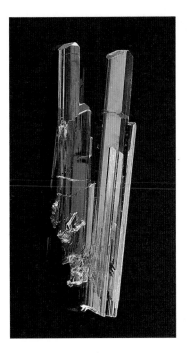

Epidote
Untersulzbachtal, Austria
24 cm (9 ⅜ in.) across

Hardystonite (Buff) with Calcite (White) and Willemite (Brown)
Franklin, New Jersey
23 cm (9 in.) across

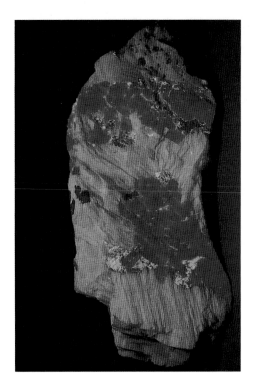

Same specimen illuminated with short wave ultra-violet light:
Hardystonite (Violet) with Calcite (Pink) and Willemite (Green)

Franklin, New Jersey

23 cm (9 in.) across

Benitoite (Blue) with Neptunite (Black) in Natrolite
San Benito County, California
4 cm (1¾ in.) across

Ferro-Axinite
Puva, Polar Urals, Russia
9.3 cm (3⅝ in.) across

Beryl (the "Patricia Emerald")
Chivor Mine, Colombia
Crystal 6.6 cm (2 ⅗ in.) high

Beryl (Variety Emerald)
Takovaya, Ural Mountains, Russia
Crystal 6.5 cm (2½ in.) high

Beryl (Variety Aquamarine) on Albite
Near Dusso, Gilgit, Pakistan
Crystal 8 cm (3 ⅛ in.) long

Beryl (Variety Aquamarine) with Albite
Dusso, Gilgit, Pakistan
Crystal 7.5 cm (3 in.) long

Beryl (Variety Aquamarine) with Fluorapatite
Dusso, Gilgit, Pakistan
8.9 cm (3½ in.) across

Beryl (Variety Morganite) with Albite, Elbaite, and Lepidolite
Tourmaline King Mine, Pala, California
22.5 cm (11 in.) across

Beryl (Variety Morganite)
Nuristan, Afghanistan
6.5 cm (2½ in.) across

Beryl (Variety Heliodor)
Minas Gerais, Brazil
Crystal 10 cm (4 in.) high

Bicolored Elbaite Tourmaline Crystals
Himalaya Mine, Mesa Grande, California
Largest crystal 10 cm (4 in.)

Elbaite (Variety Rubellite)
Tourmaline with Microcline and Albite
Himalaya Mine, Mesa Grande, California
Crystal 25 cm (10 in.) long

Elbaite (Variety Rubellite) Tourmaline in Quartz
Himalaya Mine, Mesa Grande, California
Crystal 5.5 cm (2⅛ in.) long

Elbaite (Variety Verdelite) Tourmaline
Himalaya Mine, Mesa Grande, California
5.3 cm (2 in.) long

Elbaite (Variety Rubellite) with Lepidolite
Stewart Mine, Pala, San Diego County, California
10 cm (4 in.) high

"Blue Cap" Elbaite Tourmaline
Tourmaline Queen Mine, Pala, San Diego County, California
10.5 cm (4 ⅛ in.) high

Elbaite Tourmaline with Morganite Beryl
Tourmaline Queen Mine, Pala, San Diego County, California
10 cm (4 in.) high

Elbaite (Variety Rubellite) Tourmaline with Quartz
Pala Chief Mine, Pala, San Diego County, California
Crystal 20.5 cm (8 in.) high

Elbaite Tourmaline Crystals
Mt. Mica, Paris, Oxford County, Maine
Crystal (first gem tourmaline found in U.S.) set in watch charm
2.2 cm (⅞ in.) long

"Watermelon" Elbaite Tourmaline with Lepidolite and Albite
Plumbago Gem Pit, Newry, Maine
22.5 cm (8 ⅞ in.) high

"Watermelon" Elbaite Tourmaline
Mawi, Nuristan, Afghanistan
23 cm (9 in.) long

"Bicolor" Elbaite Tourmaline
Mawi, Nuristan, Afghanistan
17 cm (6 ¾ in.) long

Elbaite Tourmaline
Alto Ligonha, Mozambique
7.3 cm (2 ⅞ in.) long

Elbaite with Albite
Stak Nala, Gilgit Division, Pakistan
6.5 cm (2½ in.) across

Polished Slice of Elbaite with Liddicoatite Rim
Anjanabonoina Mine, Antsirabe, Malagasy Republic
13.2 cm (5¼ in.) across

Schorl with Quartz and Albite
Little Three Mine, Ramona, San Diego County, California
Black crystal 4 cm (1½ in.) long

Schorl with Microcline and Quartz
Pech, Konar Province, Afghanistan
13.5 cm (5¼ in.) across

Dioptase on Calcite
Tsumeb, Namibia
8.7 cm (3⅜ in.) across

Diopside
Dekalb, New York
Crystal 7.5 cm (3 in.) long

Spodumene (Variety Kunzite)
Mawi, Nuristan, Afghanistan
8.9 cm (3½ in.) long

Spodumene (Variety Hiddenite) with Quartz and Pyrite
Hiddenite, Alexander County, North Carolina

12.5 cm (5 in.) across

Spodumene with Quartz, Norwich Pegmatite
Sterling, Massachusetts
13.5 cm (5¼ in.) across

Wollastonite (Buff) in Calcite (White)
Franklin, New Jersey
13 cm (5⅛ in.) across

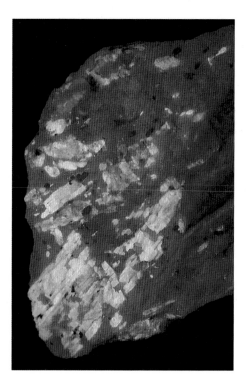

Same specimen illuminated with shortwave ultra-violet light:
Wollastonite (Pink) in Calcite (Purple-Blue)
Franklin, New Jersey
13 cm (5⅛ in.) across

Rhodonite
Franklin, New Jersey
40 cm (16 in.) across

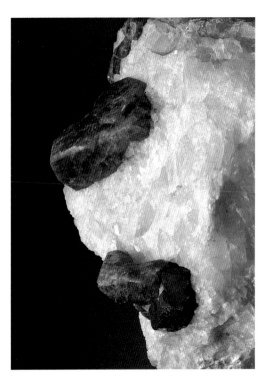

Rhodonite with Franklinite and Calcite
Franklin, New Jersey
Largest crystal 3 cm (1¼ in.) across

Actinolite (Variety Nephrite)
Largest nephrite ever recorded from Europe, weighs 2144 kg (4727 lb.)
Jordanow, Poland
On loan from the Metropolitan Museum of Art

Hornblende in Calcite
Sterling Hill Mine, Ogdensburg, New Jersey
8 cm (3 ⅛ in.) across

Muscovite Mica
Hiddenite, Alexander County, North Carolina
15.5 cm (6 in.) across

Phlogopite Micas:
Top: Ogdensburg, New Jersey; Bottom: Franklin, New Jersey
Top: 10.5 cm (4⅛ in.) across

Lepidolite Mica
Little Three Mine, Ramona, San Diego County, California
18 cm (7 in.) across

Prehnite
Lower New Street Quarry, Paterson, New Jersey
16.8 cm (6⅝ in.) across

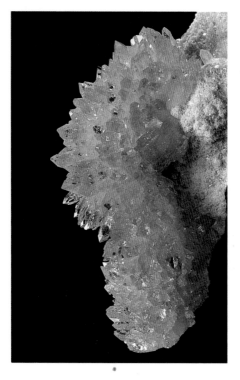

Fluorapophyllite on Rock Matrix
Poona, India
12 cm (4¾ in.) across

Bementite
Trotter Mine, Franklin Furnace, New Jersey.
9 cm (3½ in.) across

Quartz (Variety Rock Crystal)
McEarl Mine, Hot Springs, Arkansas
13.5 cm (5⅓ in.) high

Quartz (Variety Amethyst)
Thunder Bay, Ontario, Canada
7.5 cm (3 in.) across

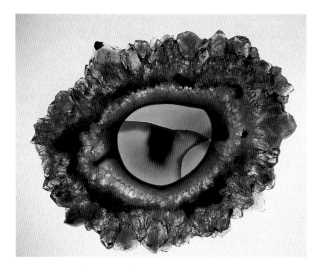

Slice of a Quartz (Variety Amethyst) Geode
Uruguay
10 cm (4 in.) high

Quartz (Variety Smoky)
Hiddenite, Alexander County, North Carolina
7.5 cm (3 in.) across

Rutilated Quartz
Itabira, Minas Gerais, Brazil
6.7 cm (2⅜ in.) across

Slice of Quartz and Moganite (Variety Agate)
Locality unknown
18 cm (7 in.) across

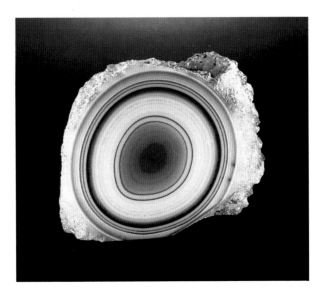

Quartz and Moganite; "Bull's Eye" Agate
Brazil
10 cm (4 in.) in diameter

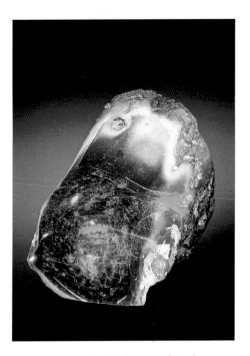

Precious Opal Replacement of Wood
Virgin Valley, Nevada
9 cm (3½ in.) long

Microcline (Variety Amazonite) with Smoky Quartz
Lake George, Teller County, Colorado
12.5 cm (5 in.) across

Polished Lapis Lazuli (Mostly Lazurite)
Oxus River, Afghanistan
13 cm (5¼ in.) high

Scapolite
Pierrepont, New York
7.5 cm (3 in.) high

Analcime with Hydroxyapophyllite
Phoenix Mine, Lake Superior, Michigan
10 cm (4 in.) across

Chabazite on Fluorapophyllite
Upper New Street Quarry, Paterson, New Jersey
9.5 cm (3 ¾ in.) across

Stilbite (Brown Sheaves) with Hydroxyapophyllite
Paterson, New Jersey
20 cm (8 in.) across

GEMS

The gems are organized by mineral species (or material), with the traditional four "precious stones" (diamonds, emeralds, rubies, and sapphires) first, followed by generally well-known gemstones with good properties (color, hardness, durability), reputation, or special pizzazz. Carving materials and lesser known gems come next, and the organic gem materials—amber, shell, pearl, and jet—are last. The commercial and fashionable nature of gems makes it impossible to organize them otherwise, unless the alphabet or the refractive index were used. Again, *de gustibus non est disputandum.* The following list shows the organization.

The "Armstrong Diamond" in a Platinum Ring with Baguettes
United States, c. 1935

14.11 carats

The "Lounsbery Diamond Necklace"

More than 100 diamonds, in rose, brilliant, pendaloque, and modified single cuts
Early 20th century; concept by Richard Lounsbery (American);
made by Cartier, Paris

Natural-Colored Diamonds from the Aurora Collection
Various sources
· Largest stone, 2 carats

The "DeLong Star Ruby"
Mogok, Myanmar (formerly Burma)
100.3 carats

The "Midnight Star Sapphire"
Sri Lanka
116.75 carats

The "Star of India"
The world's largest gem-quality blue star sapphire
Sri Lanka
563.35 carats

Sapphire (Variety Padparadscha)
Sri Lanka
100 carats

An Array of Fancy Sapphires
Sri Lanka
3.50 carats to 188 carats

Sapphires
Sri Lanka
2 to 16.9 carats

Faceted and "Rough" Sapphires
Yogo Gulch, Montana
0.75 to 2.25 carats

Rubies
Cabochon: Mogok, Myanmar (formerly Burma); 47 carats
Round: Cullakenee Mine, Clay County, North Carolina; 1.38 carats
Oval: Tanzania; 1.87 carats

The "Schettler Emerald"
Muzo, Colombia
Carved in India, c. 17th century
87.64 carats; 3.5 cm (1⅜ in.) across

Emerald and Diamond Pendant, Set in Platinum
Emerald rough, Colombia
Fashioned in Russia
1.6 cm (⅝ in.) long

Aquamarines
Crystal Fragment: Marambaia, Brazil;
5.28 kg (11.6 lb.), 48.3 cm (19 in.) across
Round Brilliant Stone: Nertchinsk, Siberia, Russia; 47.39 carats

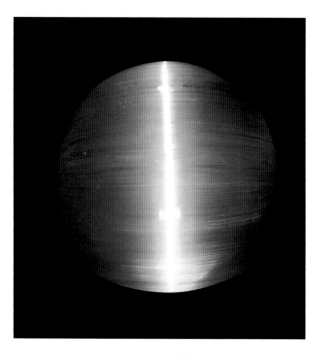

Aquamarine Cat's Eye
Minas Gerais, Brazil
145 carats

Aquamarine Necklace with Pearls, Diamonds, Platinum, Gold
United States, Edwardian style, c. 1900

**Aquamarine Brooch, Earrings, and Ring with Diamonds
in Platinum and Gold**
United States, late Art Deco style, c. 1940
Large emerald-cut stone, 41.25 carats

Aquamarine, Morganite, and Heliodor
Various sources
From 11.38 carats (emerald-cut golden heliodor)
to 390.25 carats (aquamarine)

Necklace: Aquamarine, Green Beryls, Emeralds, Rubies, Diamonds, Sapphires, Carnelian, Glass, Gold, Enamel, and Cord
Moroccan, c. 1750; part of the official trappings of the vizier
(Top inset: reverse view of central pendant)

Heliodor
Crystal: Siberia, Russia; 7.5 cm (3 in.) long
Stone: Sri Lanka; 59.01 carats

Chinese Statuette of a Goddess
Carved morganite from Anjanabonoina Mine, Antsirabe,
Malagasy Republic; c. 1920
10.5 cm (4¼ in.) high

Morganite
Anjanabonoina Mine, Antsirabe, Malagasy Republic
58.79 carats

Morganites
Square-Cut Stone: Minas Gerais, Brazil; 278.25 carats
Crystal with Bi-Color Elbaite:
Tourmaline Queen Mine, Pala, San Diego County, California
Crystal 6.5 cm (2½ in.) across

Chrysoberyls
Sri Lanka and Brazil
8.9 to 74.44 carats

Cat's Eye Chrysoberyl
Probably Sri Lanka
89.5 carats

Alexandrite (Shown with Characteristic Color Change)
Sri Lanka
8.9 carats

Spinel
Sri Lanka
70.99 carats

Spinels
Mogok, Myanmar (formerly Burma)
Octahedral Crystal in Marble, 1 cm (⅜ in.) across
Stone, 4.03 carats

Spinels
Ring with 9.5-Carat Spinel
Mogok, Myanmar (formerly Burma); Diamonds, Gold, Platinum;
United States, c. 1900
Other stones, Sri Lanka, 1.89 to 46.48 carats

The "Brazilian Princess" Topaz
Minas Gerais, Brazil
21,005 carats, 14.5 cm (5¾ in.) across

Imperial Topazes
Crystal, Ouro Preto, Minas Gerais, Brazil; 5.5 cm (2⅛ in.) long
Cut stone, Sri Lanka, 16.95 carats

Topazes
Minas Gerais, Brazil
Pink cushion-cut 47.55-carat and oval-cut Imperial 47.75-carat stones   *253*

Rare Red Topaz
Either Minas Gerais, Brazil; or Russia
70.4 carats

Topazes
Various localities
17.16 to 375 carats

Pink Elbaites
Stewart Mine, Pala, San Diego County, California
Crystal, 10 cm (4 in.) long; cut stone, 419.5 carats

Elbaites
Various localities
1.27 to 127.7 carats

Bicolored Elbaites
Mesa Grande, California
Crystals, up to 9.5 cm (3 ¾ in.) long; cabochon, 22.4 carats; cut stone,
30.5 carats

Bicolored Elbaite Carved in the Form of a Rhinoceros
Minas Gerais, Brazil; Osaka, c. 1946
8.5 cm (3⅜ in.)

Almandine Garnet Bowl
India; late 19th century (?)
Diameter 5.5 cm (2⅛ in.)

Brooch and Bracelet of Rose-Cut Bohemian Pyrope Garnets, Gilt Metal
England, c. 1875–1900

Demantoid Garnet
Poldenwaja, Ural Mountains, Russia
4.94 carats

Hessonite Engraving with Christ's Head
Sri Lanka; from the Vatican collection
Italy, 18th or 19th century
3.6 cm (1⅜ in.) high

Tsavorite Garnet
Probably Teita Hills, Kenya
Gravel and 8.16-carat stone

Rhodolite Garnet
Tanzania
24.5 carats

Spessartine Garnet
Amelia Court House, Virginia
Etched mass 6 cm (2⅜ in.) across and 98.61-carat cut stone

Garnets
Spessartine crystals on quartz, Tange-Achin, Nangarhar Province, Afghanistan;
largest 1.5 cm (⁹/₁₆ in.) across
Almandine, Tanzania; 28.41 carats
Round brilliant-cut pyrope, Macon County, North Carolina;
8.97 carats

**Pendant Set with Australian Opals, Chrysoberyl, Sapphires, Topazes,
Demantoid Garnets, and Pearls in Gold**
American, 1915–1925, designed by Louis Comfort Tiffany at Tiffany & Co.
4.5 cm (1¾ in.) long

268

"Harlequin Prince" Black Opal
Australia
215.85 carats

Opalized Clam
Coober Pedy, Australia
69 carats

Fire Opals
Queretaro, Mexico
4.72 to 31.7 carats

Opal Carving
Stuart Range, South Australia; American, c. 1929
6.3 cm (2½ in.) long

Opal Carving
Myneside, West Queensland, Australia; American, c. 1929
4.2 cm (1¾ in.) high

Ametrine (Amethyst-Citrine) (left)
Puerto Isabel, Bolivia
45.71 carats
Amethyst Brooch with Diamonds and Gold (right)
England (?), c. 1890–1900

Ametrine (Amethyst-Citrine)
Puerto Isabel, Bolivia
45.71 carats

Amethysts
Ural Mountains, Russia
163.5 carats (left) and 88.2 carats (right)

"Pinwheel" Amethyst
Brazil
41.17 carats

Quartzes, Including Rock Crystal, Smoky Quartz, Citrine, Amethyst, Green Quartz, and Rose Quartz
Various localities
13.16 to 489.85 carats

Crucifixion Pendant with Rock Crystal, Pearl, Gold, and Enamel
Spain, 17th century
3.8 cm (1½ in.) long

Rock Crystal Carving of a Horse Head
Russia, late 19th century
13.2 cm (5¼ in.) high

Rock Crystal Carving of Atlas Supporting the Earth
Ural Mountains, Russia, 19th century
12 cm (4⅝ in.) high

Tiger Eye Quartz Carving of Buddha
Prieska, N. Cape Province, South Africa; Chinese, early 20th century

8 cm (3 ⅛ in.) high

Peridot
Zabargad Island, Egypt
Crystal, 4.1 cm (1⅝ in.) long; cut stone, 10.92 carats

Peridots
Top stone, Myanmar (formerly Burma); 164.16 carats
Other stones, Zabargad Island, Egypt; 95.19 carats and 61.55 carats

Peridot
From the meteorite, Eagle Station, Kentucky
0.52 carats

Zircons
Sri Lanka and Thailand
7.76 to 40.19 carats

Zircon
Thailand
The world's largest known gem zircon
Brilliant-cut, 208.65 carats

Turquoises
High cabochon, Iran; 93.98 carats
Spider-web cabochon, Santa Rita, New Mexico; 90.2 carats

Turquoise Buddhist Lion
Chinese carving, material from Tibet
6.1 cm (2 ⅜ in.) long

Variscite Sphere, Two Cabochons, and Cabochon Gold Pin
Fairfield, Utah
Sphere, 7.5 cm (2¹⁵⁄₁₆ in.)

Lapis Lazuli Chinese Junk
15.2 cm (6 in.) high

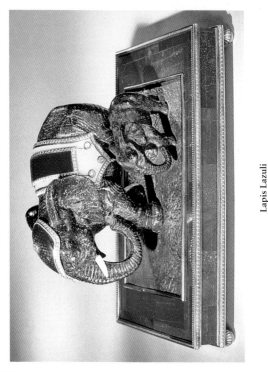

Lapis Lazuli

Fabergé Carving of Russian Material Decorated with Sterling Silver, Yellow Gold, Red and Yellow Enamel, and Small Rose-Cut Diamonds

16 cm (6 ¼ in.) across

292

Labradorites
Clear Lake, Oregon
2.09 to 3.01 carats

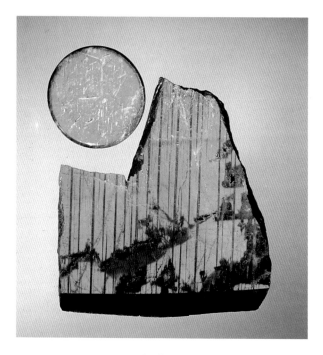

Labradorites
Labrador, Canada
Disk diameter, 3.2 cm (1¼ in.)

Microclines (Variety Amazonite)
Crystal, Lake George area, Colorado, 6 cm (2 ⅜ in.) across
Floral cabochons, Amelia Court House, Virginia

Moonstone Intaglios of Four Siblings, Set with Pearls and Platinum;
American, c. 1930
Carved by Ottavio Negri; Moonstone from Sri Lanka
(average, 2 cm [¾ in.] high)
Central image enlarged

Jadeite Jade Incense Burner
Chinese, late 19th century; Burmese jade
18 cm (7 in.) high

Jadeite Jade Statuette of Kwan-yin
Chinese, late 19th century; Burmese jade
28 cm (12½ in.) high

Jadeite Jade
Nine small cabochons; Myanmar (formerly Burma)
Two large stones; Guatemala, 6.38 to 28.34 carats,
on jadeite jade boulder from Myanmar

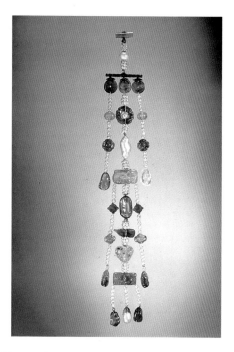

Headdress Pendant with Imperial Jadeite Jade, Pearls, Sapphires, Pink
Tourmalines, and Cord

Chinese, c. 1900

Nephrite Jade Bi (Disk of Heaven)
Ming dynasty
31 cm (12¼ in.) across

Nephrite Jade Water Buffalo Carving
Ming dynasty
27 cm (10½ in.) long

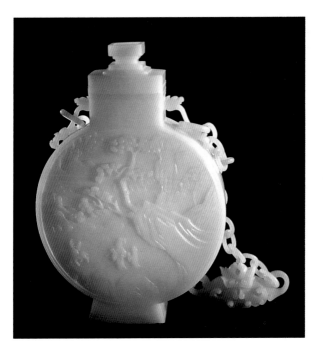

Nephrite Jade Hanging Vase
Chinese (Qianlong), 18th century
18 cm (8 1/16 in.) high

Serpentine Vase
Chinese (Qianlong) (?), 18th century; material from Mongolia
16.7 cm (6¾₁₆ in.) high

Chalcedony; "Pas de Danse"
G. Tonnelier, Paris, c. 1900; material from Uruguay
21.5 cm (8½ in.) high

Moss Agate
India
Largest 7.5 (3 in.) in diameter

Chalcedony Vase
China
10.6 cm (4¼ in.) high

Onyx Clock Face
German, carved cameo style, 1867
Diameter 11.5 cm (4½ in.)

Carnelian Vase
Chinese
14.5 cm (4 ⅛ in.) across

Agate Cameo
Material from Uruguay
4.7 cm (1⅞ in.) high

Carnelian

Islamic Necklace with Red Tassels

Chinese Belt Buckle, 6 cm (2⅜ in.) across

17th century Merovingian necklace, 28 cm (11 in.) across

Native American Bead Bracelets

Rhodochrosite
N'Chwaning Mine, Kuruman, N. Cape Province, South Africa
Crystals 7 cm (2 ¾ in.) across; stone, 59.65 carats

Benitoite

San Benito County, California

Stone, 3.57 carats; crystal with neptunite in natrolite,
2 cm (¾ in.) across

Amblygonite
Linopolis, Minas Gerais, Brazil

Stone, 34 carats; crystal, 8 cm (3⅛ in.) high

Malachite Vase
China, 18th or 19th century
20 cm (7 ⅞ in.) high

Malachite Carving of the God of Happiness
China, late 19th century (?)
10 cm (4 in.) high

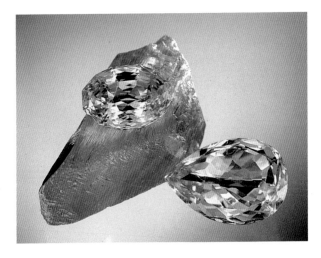

Spodumene (Variety Kunzite)
Pala Chief Mine, Pala, San Diego County, California
Crystal, 9.8 cm (3 ¹³⁄₁₆ in.) long;
two cut stones, 121.48 and 191.84 carats

Titanite
10.07-carat stone, Switzerland
Twinned crystal, Austria, 5.5 cm (2⅛ in.) long

Euclase
Crystals, Zimbabwe; largest 5.5 cm (2⅛ in.) long
Cut stones, Minas Gerais, Brazil; 7.94 carats and 8.64 carats

Calcite

Gallatin County, Montana

Crystal, 7.3 cm (2 ⅞ in.) long; stone, 99.6 carats

West Indian Emperor Helmet Shell Cameo; "Chariot of the Muses"
Italian, late 19th century
11.5 cm (9 in.) across

Oyster Shell with Mother-of-Pearl Buddhas
(The oyster covered lead implants with nacreous shell)
About 11 cm (5 in.) across

"Ammolite" (Fossilized Ammonite)
Northern Alberta, Canada
18.3 cm (7⅛ in.) across; cabochons, 9.67 carats and 41.98 carats

Carving of Mediterranean Coral
Chinese, 19th century
35.6 cm (14 in.) high

Amber
Chinese carving, early 20th century; 10.9 cm (4¼ in.) high
Beads, Baltic Coast
Polished piece, Sicily; 11.5 cm (4½ in.) long

Amber Dress Ornament
Chinese carving, 19th century (?), material from Myanmar (formerly Burma)

7 cm (2 ¾ in.) long

Fresh-Water Pearls
Various U.S. rivers
Shell 9.5 cm (3 ¾ in.) across

Triton Pendant with Baroque Pearl, Pearls, Ruby, Gold, and Enamel
Italian, mid-19th century, Renaissance revival style

5 cm (2 in.) long

Jet
Slab, 9.5 cm (3 ¾ in.) long
Faceted stone, 2.92 carats; cabochon 5.26 carats; unknown localities
Frog with turquoise, Chaco Cañon, New Mexico; 8.1 cm (3 ⁷⁄₁₆ in.) high
(from the Department of Anthropology)

Various Ornamental Stones

Heliotrope (bloodstone) cylinder; banded jasper cabochon; carnelian pendant, 6 cm (2 ⅜ in.) high; faceted blue chalcedony; obsidian bowl; onyx intaglio; sodalite, prehnite, turquoise, and jadeite cabochons

INDEX

Page numbers in *italic* refer to illustrations.

PHOTOGRAPHY CREDITS

The photographers and the sources of photographic material, by page number, are as follows;
some photographs have a joint credit.

SELECTED **TINY FOLIOS**™ FROM ABBEVILLE PRESS

- American Impressionism 1-55859-801-4 ▪ $10.95
- Audubon's Birds of America:
  The Audubon Society Baby Elephant Folio 1-55859-225-3 ▪ $10.95
- The Great Book of Currier & Ives' America 1-55859-229-6 ▪ $10.95
- The Great Book of French Impressionism 1-55859-336-5 ▪ $10.95
- Norman Rockwell: 332 Magazine Covers 1-55859-224-5 ▪ $10.95
- The North American Indian Portfolios:
  Bodmer, Catlin, McKenney & Hall 1-55859-601-1 ▪ $10.95
- Treasures of Folk Art 1-55859-560-0 ▪ $11.95
- Treasures of Impressionism and Post-Impressionism:
  National Gallery of Art 1-55859-561-9 ▪ $11.95
- Treasures of the Louvre 1-55859-477-9 ▪ $11.95
  French-language edition: 2-87946-033-6
- Treasures of the Musée D'Orsay 1-55859-783-2 ▪ $11.95
  French-language edition: 1-55859-043-3
  Japanese-language edition: 1-55859-883-9
- Treasures of the Musée Picasso 1-55859-836-7 ▪ $11.95
  French-language edition: 1-55859-044-1
  Japanese-language edition: 1-55859-884-7
- Treasures of 19th- and 20th-Century Painting:
  The Art Institute of Chicago 1-55859-603-8 ▪ $11.95
- Treasures of the Prado 1-55859-558-9 ▪ $11.95
  Spanish-language edition: 1-55859-654-2
- Treasures of the Uffizi 1-55859-559-7 ▪ $11.95
- Wild Flowers of America 1-55859-564-3 ▪ $10.95